BEND
TO
BAJA

A BIOFUEL POWERED SURFING AND CLIMBING ROAD TRIP

BEND
TO
BAJA

A BIOFUEL POWERED SURFING AND CLIMBING ROAD TRIP

JEFF**JOHNSON**

stellar

BOULDER, COLORADO

Printed in China on recycled paper.

10 9 8 7 6 5 4 3 2 1

International Standard Book Number:
ISBN 10: 0-9723422-9-X
ISBN 13: 978-09723422-9-2

Library of Congress Cataloging-in-Publication
Data applied for.

Distributed to the bookseller trade by
Publishers Group West.

Design: Mike Slone
Editor: Philip Drake
Publisher: Stellar Transmedia

Moonlight Publishing LLC
2528 Lexington Street
Lafayette, CO 80026 USA
www.moonlight-publishing.com

stellar
LIFESTYLE BY ADVENTURE

Stellar Transmedia LLC
1209 Pearl Street Suite 11
Boulder, CO 80302
stellartransmedia.com

Stellar Books is an imprint of Moonlight Publishing.

patagonia®

the cleanest line

patagonia.com   800 638 6464

Patagonia and Stellar are both
members of 1% For The Planet.
Learn more at:
www.OnePercentForThePlanet.org.

Contents

FOREWORD

In the long gone days of the Silver Dons, the hardscrabble constituents of the far west often referred to "the three Californias." These were Alta California, Baja California, and Baja Sur, comprising the area between the brackish lagoon of San Jose del Cabo in the south and the bayside pueblo of San Francisco to the north.

This land was unimaginably rich, and thoughtfully stewarded by the bands of indios who lived within its unmarked borders. While it's widely held that the region went to hell the moment Cabrillo and the rest of the Euros hit, that's not entirely true. From about 1550 to 1960—nearly half a millennia—the Three Californias remained fertile ground for adventure and opportunity. These days, one must root through the duff like a truffle pig to find the nuggets. It's a game requiring cunning, resolve, and scholarship. And while the World Wide Web's insidious tentacles are definitely giving up secrets, the true gems are still passed from man to man:

"Try St. Annes on a small West wind swell…"

"Check Officers' during a steep South, five-plus high tide, and a North wind…"

"The kooks don't know that Newb will break on the right SW…"

Beyond that, simply balling the jack down the 101 with a truck full of grub and boards offers up that most sacred of gems: surprise.

That's what author Jeff Johnson and company were looking for. Ventura was the start-point, and they scored the best waves of the trip right under their noses between San Buenaventura and Punta Mugu. Thus refreshed, they smoked north to Smith Rock and the high chaparral of Bend, Oregon. Climbed-out, they plunged back down the coast, rinsing off the road grease at Fort Point and in the pocket coves near San Francisco.

More savories were yet to come.

In a deep Baja valley lousy with quail, a graded dirt road offered up a sort of time travel. It was an hour or two to the sandstone bluffs, but decades melted away with each mile of washboard. This is the land of the four-strand reata and sweating cans of Tecate, the beige martini of the ejido class. Pangueros sculled their craft over the eelgrass, waiting for lulls so they could dart out to hookah dive the urchin beds. An osprey dropped like a Stuka, absolutely drilling a small calico bass drawn by the sun to the surface. Whiteface cattle chewed benignly on the coastal mesas. Time stood still.

While the clan shown in this volume continued down to the Tip, the tableau described strikes an emblematic note. They hit a south swell spot in the off-season, and there it was. Nothing earth shattering, wave wise. Just the comfort of friends and the dignity of space. Fresh halibut, smoky reposado tequila, and plenty of time to learn the 195 Castilian words for the colors of horses.

—Scott Hulet
San Clemente, 2006

PREFACE

I was 14 years old and had just run away from home. I woke up under a house, staring at pink fiberglass insulation and a floor joist, on an old mattress in the dirt. The morning sun sifted through a vent in the cement foundation, illuminating my high-top Vans and my dirty clothes stacked carefully on top of them. I heard a door slam, a car start and drive away, a dog barking. A beat up ghetto blaster turned on, and the Angry Samoans blared through the house—my friend's cue that it was safe for me to come upstairs.

This was the first morning of what turned out to be five long days of perilous endeavors—my first taste of travel and adventure. I was both scared and excited at having put myself out into the unknown. For the first time in my life, I was free to do whatever I wanted. That week my accomplice and I saw a few punk bands play in Berkeley (a town forbidden to me). By day, I wandered aimlessly, by night I skated through city streets like an outlaw. I stayed out late (no curfew), ate whatever I wanted, and came and went as I pleased. Yet, things weren't so easy. After being humbled by the realities of being a "free" kid in the real world, I went home with my tail between my legs. It was this combined sense of freedom, humility, and curiosity about things beyond my grasp that formed the way I approach the world.

As I revisit the photographs and journal entries from our six-week road trip from Bend to Baja, I see faces and places that share a certain quality. It is this quality that I've been chasing since I was 14 years old. I hope you enjoy this book of interpretations.

–Jeff Johnson
Ventura, 2006

Cool 'n   8th Grade

Introduction

I first met the Malloy brothers, Chris, Keith, and Dan, in the mid '90's while living on the North Shore of Oahu, Hawaii. It started with random encounters at remote surf spots and quickly evolved to lofty talk at crowded house parties. Having similar interests, and a wealth of mutual friends, we hit it off.

Eventually, the four of us shared a beachside house at Rocky Point. Soon thereafter, we found ourselves together on surf trips to faraway places like Tahiti, Australia, and Indonesia. Our paths were dialed.

After more than a decade of this, while hanging out in their hometown of Ventura, California, the Malloy's and I had a small revelation: we knew more about places like Rantuaprapat, Sumatra, and Bonduran, Ireland, than we did the west coast of California, where we were born and raised. This had to be remedied. An extended road trip was the call: surfing, climbing, and camping the entire way.

First, we would travel north from Ventura to Bend, Oregon, then make a 180-degree turn south to cover 2,000 long miles down the Pacific Coast to the tip of Baja. We invited a diverse traveling crew, and friends could join for any leg of the trip. Keith and I would stay together for the duration, and Chris and Dan planned to come along for a healthy serving.

A few months before the trip, Keith bought a used diesel truck. He was instantly concerned about its lack of fuel economy and began searching for alternatives. One day, while having lunch at local cafe, he saw an intriguing posting. On the bulletin board between lost dogs and rooms for rent was a flyer promoting biodiesel, vegetable oil, and ways to convert vehicles to run on alternative fuel sources. With a stroke of inspiration, Keith disappeared into the hills of Ojai and spent long hours outfitting his rig at mechanic Joel Woolf's ranch. When he re-emerged, we had a truck that could run on cooking grease and biodiesel, which made our consciences (and wallets) much happier.

And just like that, with our shit seemingly in order, we snuck out of Ventura one winter's day in late February 2005 and hit the open road. What follows is a record of our six-week journey.

01

California North

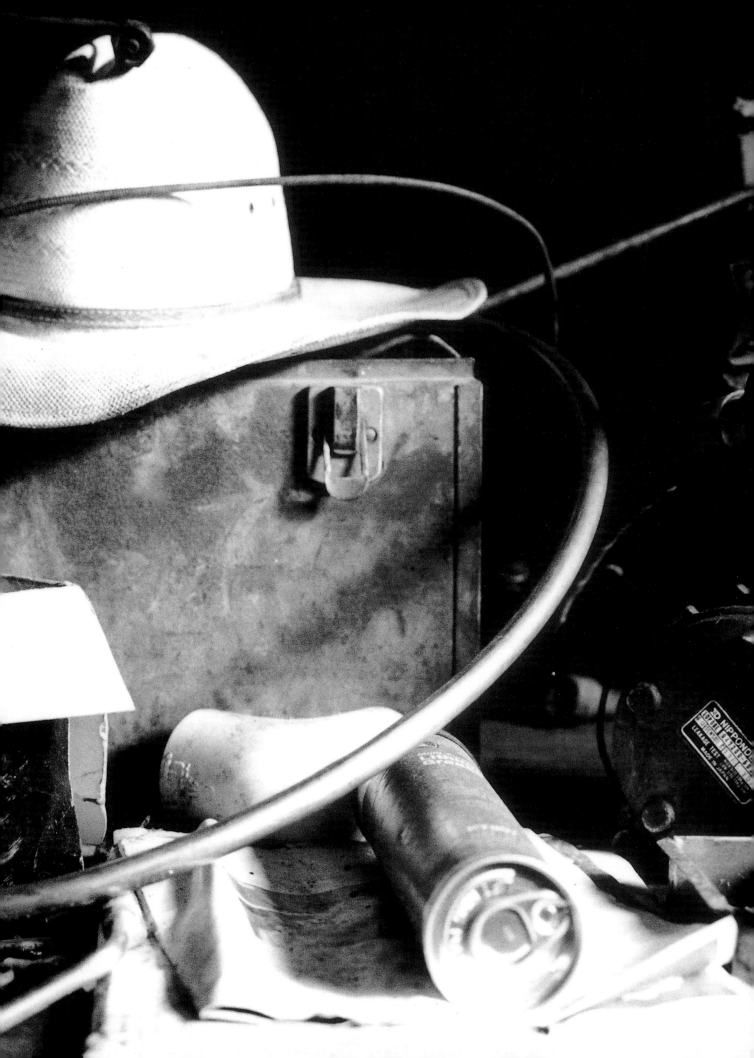

In 1894, inventor Rudolf Diesel filed a patent for an internal combustion engine known as the diesel engine. It was designed to run on peanut oil, a biofuel. These days virtually every diesel engine can run on biodiesel without being modified. However, to run on pure vegetable oil, a separate veggie tank and alternate fuel lines must be installed.

▲ Expert veggie mechanic Joel Woolf walks Keith Malloy through the installation process. Before the trip, Keith spent two weeks on Joel's small ranch wrenching his engine and getting covered in grease. His labor was well worth it. During our six-week road trip we were able to burn veggie oil and biodiesel, which reduced our emissions considerably.

▲   Joel, his wife, Rebecca, and their two dogs, Garth and Janie.

◀   Joel teaches Keith the proper technique for straining vegetable oil.

Northbound on the 101 in Ventura County, the first 25 minutes of the trip. This was the wettest winter in some twenty years, which caused major floods and traffic jams. Searching for an escape route, we were able to access old, muddy agriculture roads to bypass the congestion.

MAVERICKS

On the first leg of our trip, we pulled into San Francisco around midnight. While driving around Ocean
Beach, in a Chinese/Irish neighborhood, we found an
old "Irish" bar on Noriega Avenue. Keith pulled into
one of a long row of empty parking stalls and switched
the motor off. It was dead quiet. No one was around.
Street lamps projected light down through the fog like
lampshades. Everything was damp and glistening. We
stepped onto the shiny sidewalk, our footsteps crisp
in the thick air. Nestled tightly between two storefronts
we found a raw plywood swinging door. Above it was
a hand-painted sign that read Flanahan's. We weren't
sure if the joint was open, and not really sure if it was
a bar. Keith pushed through the door and I followed.

As we entered, I was immediately tempted to leave.
The inside was brightly lit and empty—save for an
old guy mopping the floor and the bartender. I had
expected a bar with some sort of "Irishness", perhaps
a girl or two, or at least a few talk-worthy drunks ram-
bling off into darkness. Instead, there was no music,
no Guinness, no Murphy's Stout, no Boddington's.

"At least the place is dirty," I said. "OK then. Two shots
of Jameson's, two Sierra Nevadas. Cheers, Keith.
Here's to swimmin' with bow-legged women."

The next morning, stepping into The Sea Biscuit,
we could see large green peaks feather and throw
behind grassy sand dunes three blocks away. We
sat drinking coffee with our friends Eddie Donnellan
and writer/surfer Daniel Duane. "Maybe Mavericks,"
someone suggested. Eddie began making phone
calls. I nervously rubbed my hands together. After a
short talk on his cell phone Eddie said with a grin,
"It's breaking." I sat with sweaty palms, while my foot
tapped against the floor. It had been a while since I'd
seen good-sized surf.

In years past I've tried the classic Waimea to Mavericks run, but never scored. On most trips the waves
didn't fully materialize, but I do remember driving past
Devil's Slide just in time to see a single wave stretch
the entire length of Montera Beach, closing it out. It
looked like Keiki Beach on Oahu's North Shore during
solid twenty-foot swell—thick, dark brown trenches.
A knot formed in my stomach. A short time later, on

Keith, myself, and Dan Duane in Mavericks parking lot. ▲

the bluff at Pillar Point, we stood watching waves far out at sea heave top to bottom, with a light northwest wind on our faces. "Shit," I said with a bit of relief. "Onshore winds..."

But this day was different. You could see Montera wasn't that big, and it was sunny and warm with a light east wind. The tide was too high now, but would drop throughout the day. Here I was on the bluff again, six or eight years after my last try. Keith was already paddling out. Clean, blue-green lumps undulated beneath the hazy horizon—arching their rounded backs as they approached, feathering lightly, backing off, and then unloading on the inside in front of the rocks. I suddenly felt weak, and not because I hadn't surfed in a long time. I could think of a million excuses. I get this way sometimes. Looking at these monsters can make me feel so insignificant, so powerless. It's humbling.

Nevertheless, psyched, I suited up, and ran down the trail to water's edge. Keith's older brother, Chris, once explained how paddling out on the lefts is a bit more exciting than the channel. He likened it to one of his favorite outer-reef entries on the North Shore. I decided to give it a go. I remembered Chris saying something about running and jumping off a shelf, then paddling like mad to make it through some double-ups. The tide was really high, and I didn't see a shelf, so I simply stepped off the sand and began paddling north. I tried to punch my 9'6" through the first suck-out and got rattled. I wrestled with my board, went for another one, and WHAM! I was behind the rocks in the turbulent estuary going out the proper channel—amidst confusing cross-currents, fluffy chunks of brown foam, and large, unorganized pyramid chop. I was instantly fueled by raw energy.

You never forget your first day at a classic spot. You've seen the photos and videos, read the stories– now you're here. The experience takes a few minutes to set in. Then it feels like you've been at the break forever. In the open channel I paddled slowly past the famous boneyard: Sail Rock, Mushroom Rock, and everything in between. Mike Parsons, Brock Little, Flea, and Jeff Clark all had epics here, and I'm sure there have been others we'll never hear of. Outside I saw Keith paddle for a wave. It lifted, feathered, and sank, not letting him in. The thing flattened out, drawing more water off the reef, and I saw a lip form halfway up the face. Slowly, it jacked and warbled, forming an unrideable doubled-up mutant—not just a big wave, but a crazy wave. I sat up on my board and listened to the explosion. I thought of Mark Foo, who died on a day much like this– sunny, clean, and not too big. I gave him my regards and paddled on.

When Mavericks first came onto the scene, and then became *the scene*, the debate was over what's heavier, Mavericks or Waimea? It only takes one session at Ocean Beach in a wetsuit and booties to answer that question. The elements don't help and all that rubber restricts movement. The cold zaps your strength and hinders your ability to hold your breath. The dark visuals alone while caught inside or shoved down deep have strong effects. Your blood pumps faster, which reduces oxygen supply. Half the battle with big waves is staying calm.

Keith. ▲

▲ An unidentified local charger.

I reached the lineup and paddled over a few waves. It seemed like a wave field—vast, like Sunset Beach. Save two other guys, we were alone out there. I was unclear where to sit. Eventually, I paddled for one. The wave reared up on a reef, coaxing me farther outside—then it warbled, lurching upward. I spun around, dug in, and committed. The offshores strengthened as the swell lifted me. I saw some very large boils sweep up the face. I pushed up, and the wave flattened out, sliding me down its back. Quietly the wave moved on, rearing its shoulders farther inside, cresting in places I hadn't imagined it would. Not so straightforward, I thought. This will take some time.

"That's how it is on high tide," said local charger Mark Alfaro, one of the two locals out there. "It'll get better as the tide drops."

He was right. As the tide dropped, the waves became more consistent and predictable. The wind also picked up. We snatched a few good ones before a small crowd trickled out for the lower tide, and even with the side-shore wind, the waves maintained their shape.

When the first videos of Mavericks circulated, we saw guys winging themselves over the falls, over and over, making the place look impossible. But it wasn't the waves that made the challenge so much as lack of experience and the short history of the place. Up to that point, California didn't have much of a big-wave history– big waves and ten-foot guns were reserved for Hawaii. If anyone from California had a 9'6" or a 10'0", it was left on the North Shore of Oahu in someone's rafters. Now there's a big-wave culture here in Northern California. Local shapers are making beautiful boards—boards that aren't collecting dust anymore. Boards being ridden well. On this day I was impressed by the high level of surfing. Local guys were charging with refined skill, casual and confident. The scene was refreshing.

Over the last few years I had lost interest in Mavericks. It seemed too crowded and so damn scary. I told Chris about this and he said, "You'll paddle out there, find a classic group of guys, a really fun wave, and you'll be hooked. It does that to you. The place is magic." I reckon he was right.

▲ (previous page)

I never wanted to be a surf photographer. I like to surf more than I like photographing it. But like most things, you give it a try, see some decent results, and it can become an obsession. Right before this trip I got my first water housing and a 600mm lens. "I'll give it a go," I thought. The first day of the trip we ended up at Mavericks. I had always dreamed of surfing there. Hmmm, what to do? I talked my good friend Eddie Donnellan into shooting the 600 from the cliff while Keith and I surfed. Not the best start.

As you can see, Eddie killed it. Keith's first wave of the session.

◄ Joyriding on California Street, San Francisco. Little did I know there was a cop car behind us for an entire block. He pulled us over, yelling at me to get off the roof and for us to follow him. When he accelerated through a yellow light, we lagged behind—Keith didn't want to break the law. We never saw him again.

▲ North Beach. We scoured the city looking for used veggie oil. It wasn't as easy to find as we had thought. Later we learned there are companies in the Bay Area that collect and sell veggie oil for use as fuel. Instead we took to the alleys.

▲ Keith found countless oil drums, but all were empty.

After searching for oil one afternoon, we pulled over to scout Fort Point under the Golden Gate Bridge. The tide was going out, and some swell was showing: fun, head-high lefts, glassy and protected by the wind. Normally I don't consider surfing in an urban environment beautiful, but this session was. The bridge creaked and groaned overhead, the old fort stood guard on the point, the current drained through the bay, and fog shrouded the Marin headlands. Fort Point is one of the most unusually aesthetic surf spots on earth.

Keith.

▲ The morning coffee ritual with a diminishing swell on the horizon.

The sun set without ceremony as the truck bobbed down a dark coastal road, passing farms and small outpost towns. We'd spent a long day in the ocean. Keith and I needed sleep. At a spot that seemed good enough, Keith pulled off the road and backed the rig into a small gully lined with ice plant. He killed the lights and the engine, and we stepped out onto dirt. We could hear waves pounding against the cliff below.

I turned the stereo up and left the doors wide open. Keith grabbed some beers and his guitar and settled onto the tailgate. Under a full yellow moon we sat for hours, listening to the surf between songs, laughing at ourselves while our tired eyes tried to focus on swell lines that marched silently across the moonlit sea.

Standing at the base of the gully I turned on my headlamp and bent over to look at a peculiar plant. "Keith," I said, "Check this out."

"What is it?" he asked, leaving the tailgate and switching on his headlamp.

"Not sure, but I have an idea."

Keith got about three feet away and started yelling. "Ahhhh! We're surrounded by poison oak! Look, it's everywhere! Ahhhh!"

As if the poison oak was chasing him, Keith grabbed his sleeping bag, jumped into the back of the truck screaming, "No! Poison oak! We're fucked!"

After slamming the tailgate closed I could still hear him.

I slept well on the crunchy ice plant. Occasionally I'd hear a truck drive by, its headlights dancing on the bluffs above like shadows from a campfire. The next 24 hours were filled with paranoiac itching, but somehow we escaped the death rash.

◀ Keith at one of many roadside attractions.

Ice plant proved to be the most ▶
comfortable bivy of the trip.

▲ Keith: shark bait.

We drove down the coast to Santa Cruz to pick up our friend, artist Elissa Pfost, who would join us on the trip. On the way, we found a well-hidden cove. The spot wasn't that good for board riding, but it was one of the best bodysurfing waves we'd ever seen.

Keith: another fruitless search for veggie oil. ▶

SAN FRANCISCO GOING NORTH

Keith and I woke up separately in strange houses, in strange rooms, in a strange part of the city. The night had begun in the Marina district at some L.A.-style sushi bar. All the girls trying to be like Paris Hilton or Britney Spears. Hideous. Somebody mentioned the Mission district, and the next thing I knew we were at a place called Delirium playing pinball, shots of tequila in our hands, surrounded by graffitied walls, dark, mysterious corners, and grime. The music was all-time: Meat Puppets, Dead Kennedys, Johnny Cash, X, Motorhead, Metallica, D.O.A, Black Sabbath, and Neil Young.

Four am came like a train wreck, and we were awake a few hours later. Eventually we wound our way back to Ocean Beach and ate greasy eggs at an old hotel near the Cliff House. It was Elissa's first day with us, and we had left her alone at Eddie's house the previous night. We found her on the beach: reading, running, stretching—she didn't seem to mind our absence.

Keith and I drenched our hangovers in the ocean. We surfed for hours in fun overhead waves. We had planned to take off for Oregon the next morning but instead decided to leave immediately. We packed our things and soon were on the Golden Gate Bridge going north, straight into rain. Nighttime came quickly. Desperate for a place to sleep, we finally found a campsite in Bodega Bay. It was here that I began to understand the reality of 'campsites.' It sucks to suddenly be nestled in between a bunch of RVs and beer-bonging city kids away for the weekend.

It rained hard for most the night, but the three of us slept well. We woke up early and wanted to leave. We made some coffee on the tailgate and packed our stuff. The teens a few sites down woke up, and a guy reached into his car and turned up the stereo. It was that song "Can't Touch This" by MC Hammer. The guy began gyrating around his car doing a bad show-off dance for the girls. You've got to be kidding me, I said to myself.

"Hey, buddy!" I yelled, trying to be somewhat discreet. "Turn that thing off. People are trying to sleep."

He looked at me defiantly, obviously upset, and turned it down—but only a tad.

This pissed me off. I hadn't had my coffee yet. I walked over to their site like a grumpy, derelict superhero who could throw their hip-hop asses off the planet in one fell swoop. "Look," I said, pointing a stiff finger at the dancing boy's face. "Do you have any respect? There are families here trying to sleep. Turn that shit off NOW!"

None of them would look me in the eye. The dancing boy gave me the leaky tire: "Tshhhh," rolling his eyes as he turned the stereo off.

Walking away, I suddenly felt old and mean. What was I doing?

As we drove away I thought of a similar incident. When I was around 16 years old I was skating a half pipe on a farm with a bunch of friends. After dark, it turned into a party. Being a young lightweight, I began to get a little obnoxious—making fun of people I didn't know, breaking things, etc. Suddenly, all I saw were cowboy boots, Wrangler jeans, and one massive brass belt buckle. I turned to run, but was caught by a calloused hand gripping my ear. He pulled my arm around my back into a half nelson and lifted me off the ground. Escorting me down the long dirt driveway with my feet barely touching the dirt he said, "When I was young I was a lot like you. But there was always someone like me to put an end to it."

▲ Keith and Elissa taking a much needed break from the road.

On an all-day leisurely drive, we wound our way through the lush hills of the North Coast, stopping for fuel at a biodiesel outpost/sustainable living compound where we felt like outlaws, as we had to sign legal documents before fueling. We lounged in ma and pa cafes, ate large portions of eggs and waffles, drank strong organic coffee, and noticed the makeup of the people change. The farther north you travel, the more communities become connected, more aware of their surroundings. It's not as if there are a bunch of dirty, radical hippies up here trying to get something for nothing—just good people trying to do what is right.

Heading north to Oregon.

02
Oregon

Like surfing, the climbing world is very small. Everyone is connected in one way or another. Somehow we have tapped into this parallel existence, and it can be like looking in the mirror.

It was our friend Brittany Griffith's birthday when we pulled in to Bend. Her house was filled with beer and food and an eclectic group of dirtbag climbers. Like us, they travel the world chasing seasons: Joshua Tree, Yosemite, Squamish, Bend, France, Patagonia, Chile, Argentina. Living out of their cars, crashing on couches, sleeping out in the open. It's much like surfing's Indonesia, Hawaii, Mexico, Peru, Spain, Morocco, and South Africa. The climber's medium is rock, the surfer's medium is water—but we're all after the same thing.

It's a vagabond lifestyle where you can find yourself the loneliest person alive one day, and the next surrounded by a tight network of friends. When everyone happens to be together, it's time for stories, heckling, and catching up. That night, the beers tilted 'till the wee morning hours, followed by late night munching on mystery food, drunken climbs, indoor jams, and crazy tales. Someone asked Keith to tell some scary surf stories. "Nah," he said. "'It's nothing like the stuff you do—you guys are crazy." That's Keith, always understated. Or maybe he doesn't ever get scared in the surf.

I woke up on the porch with ice on my sleeping bag, bodies all over the house, Keith and Elissa in tents in the backyard, and more bodies in bags on the frozen brown lawn. Brittany slept in her own bed where she said some guy came in late to wish her goodnight and puked all over her wall. He didn't stand a chance.

Ivo Ninov and his ▶
accomplice racking
up for a climb up the
Monkey—a prominent
500-foot feature in Smith
Rock State Park.

▲ Brittany, Ben Moon and Elissa in Ben's campervan preparing dinner.

▲ Ivo, the dirtbag golfer engages in morning shenanigans at our campsite outside of Smith Rock.

Keith is afraid of heights. He becomes really quiet. Ever since I learned of his fear, I've dragged him on a handful of great climbs. This picture is one of my favorites. His legs are dangling over hundreds of feet of air as he prepares to rappel. I can only imagine what's going through his head.

◀ A friend attempts the north face of the Monkey. 5.12a.

Keith ▶

sleeping bag
line-up

cave bivvy
smith rocks

◀ Brittany.

Morning coffee poured into empty Tecate cans 400 feet up in the Monkey cave.

All twisted in the cooking pot.

On our way to Eugene, we stopped to see our good friend Gerry Lopez. He didn't seem to mind us interrupting his work for a half-day snowboard session. Keith and Gerry discussed board design outside Gerry's shaping bay.

Keith:

To me, Gerry Lopez was special before I learned *who* he was. When I was nine years old, I didn't know what he looked like. I didn't know if he was regular or goofy-foot. I just knew if I was asked who my favorite surfer was, the best possible answer was "Gerry Lopez."

As I grew older I became more educated about Gerry. I began to understand why his name had been so in-grained in my head as a kid. I learned that he was the king of Pipeline—the first guy to make one of the heaviest waves in the world look easy, which he did with a style that couldn't be emulated, although every-one tried. After surfing Pipeline myself, the thought of riding it as Gerry did back in the seventies, on only a single fin, seemed completely impossible.

Gerry had finished surfing Pipeline before I had even reached the North Shore, so I was stoked to get the chance to go to Chile with him last year. We scored a perfect six-to-eight-foot swell and surfed until we couldn't surf any longer. I was really impressed by his skill and stamina in the water. At one point I remember surfing all day until I couldn't catch another wave, and sure enough, Gerry was still out there, in the waning light, catching the last few sets of the day. Spending time with him in Chile allowed me to see firsthand what a unique individual he is. The stories I'd heard about his strict yoga routine and clean living were true, and he also kept us entertained at dinner with his great storytelling.

When we drove through Oregon, I was hoping to catch him so we could once again be inspired. When Gerry took us snowboarding at Mount Bachelor, hours from the ocean, it was a surprise to see his popularity amongst the mountain community. And again, I was impressed by his skill on the slopes as I labored to keep up with him.

It's not often that you get to meet one of your child-hood heroes, and it's even more rare that this hero lives up to your expectations. I guess I had it right from the beginning: Gerry Lopez is a special person.

▲ Keith.   ▼ Jerry.

Master craftsman, master boardrider. Gerry's been drawing clean ▶
lines since the day he was born.

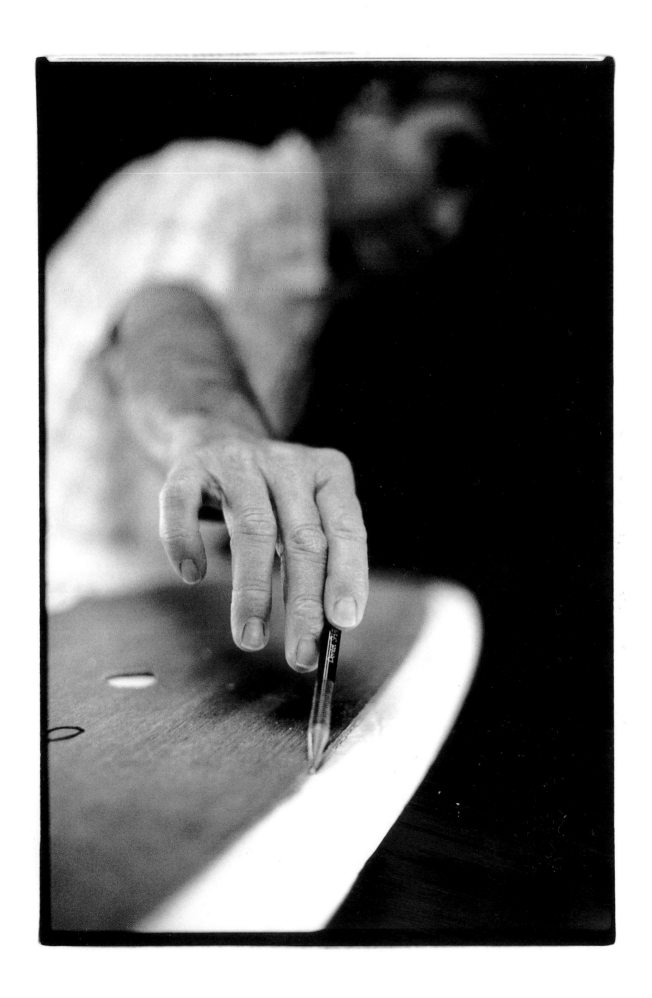

vagrancy:
the state of wandering and having no permanent place to live.

bivy:
short for the French word "bivouac," which means to sleep without shelter.

No reservations, no kiosk, no rangers, no fee, no overflowing garbage cans, and absolutely no campsite. If you have a 'site' then it's not really camping. I prefer the unplanned bivy, cowboy-style: sleep when you are tired (wherever you end up), make camp, and leave the place just as you found it. It's a shame that vagrancy is actually illegal in parts of this country. Hell, vagrancy is how this country was settled! And in some dirtbag circles, it's a compliment to be called a vagrant, the embodiment of freedom.

After snowboarding with Gerry, we asked him where we could camp. He turned to the Mount Bachelor parking attendants and asked them. "Anywhere you want," said the man, waving his hand through the air. "Hell, you can set up camp right here in the parking lot."

It turns out you can camp just about anywhere in Oregon, as long as it's public property. Makes sense, I thought. 'Public' property. This was much different than California, where it seems like every square inch of soil has a rule, a regulation, and a price.

▲ Our friend Dan Duane was beamed down through the lens flair from a flying saucer buzzing overhead. He lingered for a few seconds, then he was gone—just like that.

MTS

Keith doing morning chores. ▶

Waste? Re-fueling the veg tank on the Green Machine.

Somehow, and only through word of mouth, we learned of a guy in Bend who had veggie oil for sale. His name is Kevin Bryant or "Kevlar," to his friends. With much in common, our crew instantly hit it off. He likes to camp along the rugged Oregon coast, hunt for crab, surf isolated breaks, and climb and snowboard high peaks. He has such a passion for the natural environment that he's committed his life to making it better...and he's always open to learning new things.

Kevin and his friends figured out on their own how to convert their diesel rigs to run on veggie oil. He collects vegetable oil from local restaurants and sells it as fuel at a low price. In addition to being a self-taught veggie maestro, he's also a sustainable building contractor specializing in Rasta Block, which is made from recycled foam.

Out of goodwill, Kevin donated enough veggie oil to fill our 30-gallon tank at no charge. Turns out he'd gotten that batch of oil from a restaurant called Longboard Louie's—the same place Gerry took us for burritos the day before. It's possible that this oil was used to cook our food. We thanked him with new jackets from Patagonia, and hit the road again.

Kevin in his backyard using a homemade oil pump/strainer.

▲ The Cascade Range, near Eugene, Oregon.

heading west to eugene.

Old-growth rain forest in the McKenzie River watershed.

▲ A 'yarder' is used to extract logs from the forest once they are cut. Behind the equipment, you can see the difference between the old growth (Top) and 'second growth' (Bottom).

◄ Pollyanna Lind educates us on the inherent problems with clear-cutting the old-growth forests. She is a staunch activist who grew up in a logging town in Douglas County. It is not her goal to put loggers out of business—it's quite the opposite. She sees alternatives. She says there are financially viable 'thinning' projects underway that are actually good for the forests. This method doesn't yield the great old-growth cash crop, but it does employ more skilled loggers than clear-cutting projects.

We live in wooden houses. We use paper products. We drink water from the mountains. We eat salmon. We drive cars. We consume. We are all polluters in one way or another. As the population of the earth grows exponentially, our generation will be forced to take action and address the environmental issues that have been building for years. Running your car on vegetable oil isn't the answer, but it's a step in the right direction. You're not going to save the world by recycling beer bottles, but it helps. The words in this very book were printed on recycled paper. The point being: even though this book is itself a polluter, whenever there's an opportunity to minimize our impact, we should do the best we can.

Keith in Pollyanna's front yard in Eugene. His Pops and him built this collapsible table for filtering the veggie oil. Keith's got the process wired, but it's still a dirty job. He was covered in oil and smelled like French fries for the next two days.

▲ Elissa journals in Pollyanna's front yard. The stump she's laying on was used on an educational tour that traveled coast-to-coast, across the States. The tree rings are labeled to give perspective on the age of the tree.
For example, a ring no more than six inches from the outside is labeled: "Christopher Columbus 'discovers'
the New World." This tree had been growing for hundreds of years prior to his landing.

I woke up indoors for a change, on a floor, in a dark room, in my sleeping bag. I sat up and could see Keith's silhouette on a couch against a blue-black star filled sky. We were crashing in our bags for almost two weeks and in different places almost every night. I'd been sleeping heavily but waking often between dreams—many dreams. In a sleepy daze, I tried to discern my dreams from reality. We were in Oregon. I knew that. Eugene to be exact. Yesterday we wandered through the hills looking at virgin, old-growth forests and giant scars in the earth where the old-growth trees had been clear cut. Being from California, where most of the forests are protected, Keith and I had never seen this reality of the timber industry.

Last night Keith and I stumbled upon a bar in an old barn on some quiet side street near downtown Eugene. We indulged in Guinness, seafood jambalaya, and slices of organic pizza. A guy and girl sang Irish folk songs on a stage that looked like the manger where Jesus was born. We intended to eat quickly and go to sleep early, but we stayed in that barn instead, perched on old wooden stools for hours.

It was a dream that had woken me this morning— something about a little town in Mexico, an ape chasing me around, and someone telling me I couldn't fly. I lay back down to see what it all meant.

The slow morning of rest is all we got because now, as I write this, I'm sitting in the passenger seat of the Green Machine driving south on I-5, just having crossed the Oregon border into California. Keith is munching sunflower seeds, one fist on the wheel, the cruise control set on 75, and a mix of Willie Nelson, Waylon Jennings, Johnny Cash, and Kris Kristofferson coming through the speakers. Elissa is in the backseat napping between sessions in her journal. We'll hopefully hit San Francisco by midnight. We intended to stay in Oregon a few more days, but Keith's older brother Chris called and told us a big swell was on the way. He had a list of options for us: Mavericks (again), some mysto spots south of the Mexican border, and some other unexplored possibilities. This is the kind of stuff you'll drive 48 hours straight for.

03
California South

California's record rainfall and devastating floods in the winter of 2005 created some of the best sand bars in recent memory. Chris, as stubborn as ever, iron-legs it through an unruly section at his home break.

◀ Chris talks with Yvon Chouinard, a freethinking climbing bum/surf addict turned founder of Patagonia, Inc. This shot was taken at least two years before our trip. Ironically, they are talking about Yvon's legendary 1968 road trip, where he and some friends drove a van from Ventura, California to the tip of South America (Patagonia) to climb Mount Fitzroy.

Keith.

Passing back through Ventura allowed us to regroup and, of course, fetch a fresh batch of surfboards. The only problem: our shaper injured himself while hunting pigs. He was using a borrowed skinning knife, which doesn't have a stop-guard, and Fletcher's right hand slid down the blade, which cut tendons in his hand. He was out of the shaping room and the water for a few months. Luckily, he had a container filled with shaped blanks he'd finished just before the accident.

Fletcher Chouinard, Yvon's son, in ▶ front of his shaping room in Ventura.

▲ Keith. Muddy Tavarua?

▲ Ventura Harbor.

◀ During this banner swell, after spinning our wheels
in all directions, we found the best waves of the trip
practically in our backyard.

Keith.

▲   No man is complete without his quiver. Stored in their dad's barn, these boards collect very little dust.

▲ Keith.

Chris at home, having breakfast with inspiration. ▲

Keith finds an empty slab.

04

Northern Baja

A three-day layover in Ventura, California gave us some time to gather our bearings once again, hook up with a few more friends, and provision ourselves for the trip down south. We invited our good friend Crystal Thornburg to join us from Hawaii—she'd never been to Baja. Keith grabbed his younger brother, Dan, and his older brother, Chris, who brought his wife Carla, their two dogs, and some of the best food this side of the Appalachian. We also asked our friend Tim Nuanes, a Baja die-hard, if he wanted to go. He didn't say much. Then, right before we left, he showed up in an old beat-up truck that he'd bought just for the trip. Jonesing for mezcal, empty waves, and lobster tails, Oxnard local Ben Lemke also jumped in at the last minute. Loaded with an assortment of overflowing milk crates, shovels, tents, tables, surfboards, a new batch of veggie oil, wetsuits, and things you can hardly fathom the need for until you need them, we gunned it for the border.

Just off the jet, Crystal braves the drop in water temperature.

▲ Dan Malloy.

Crystal displays personal hygiene: a rare sight in Baja

Tim doing some ding repairs during downtime.

An unusually wet winter made Baja look more like New Zealand.

Chris and his two dogs, Major and King.

▲ Crystal.

On the backside of the point we found this funky wave that rolled along a jagged wall. As if on a slalom course, you had to negotiate your board through urchin-infested rocks. Sketchy.

▼ Ben.

▲ Dan. ▶

Dan.

Elissa, perpetually in the creative mood. ▲

▲ Crystal, as Baja life begins to settle in.

Crystal and Ben distracted by surf during dish duty. ▲

▲   Ben enjoying some solitude.

Man-grom Chris Malloy.

Yours truly.

pacific barracuda

Ben walking on air.

The view from camp.   am 3.15.05

▲ Dan sampling a bit of high tide magic.

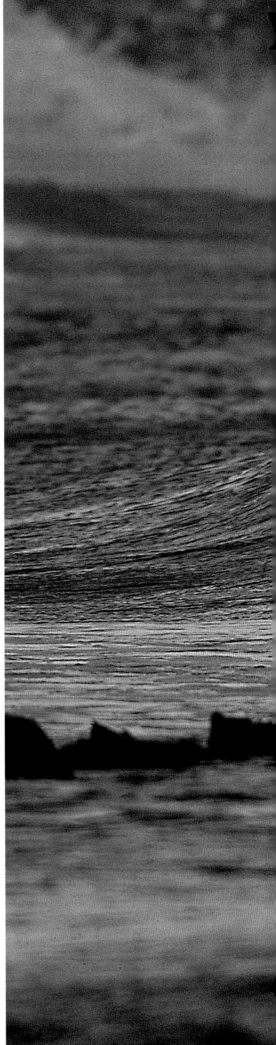

Crystal and the loo.

Dan.

Chris.

Dan.

▲ Tim.

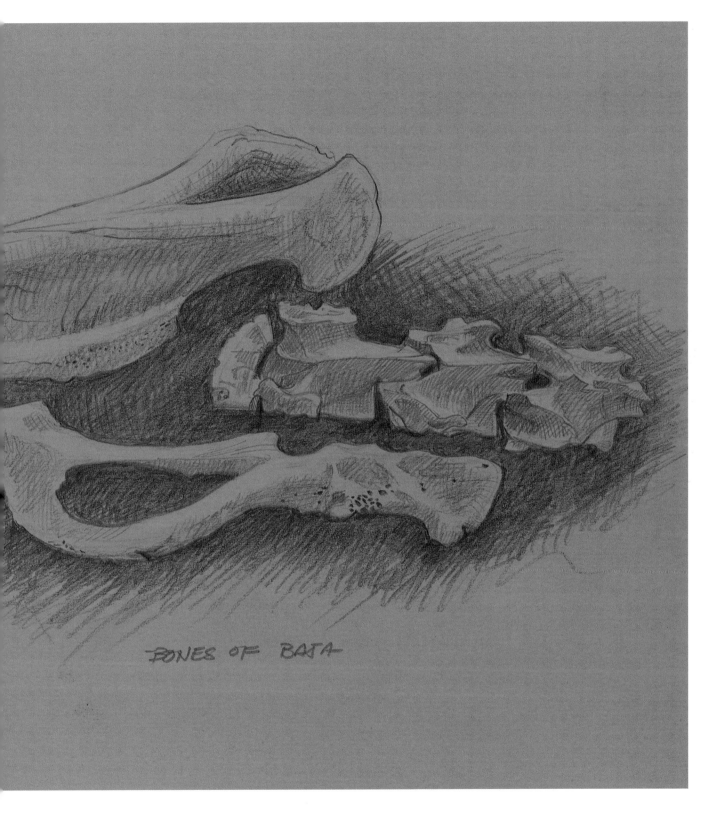

BONES OF BAJA

Elissa's art. ▲

▲ Keith.

Dan. ▲

After seven days of indulging in a freak northwest swell, perfect weather, good friends and relative solitude, the five of us decided to break off into a two-truck caravan and move farther south. Before heading into dryer climates we pulled over to smell the flowers. After an extraordinarily wet winter, it may be years before Baja sees wild flowers like this again.

Farther south.

05
Baja South

▲ Elissa's art.

near
Catavina
3...05
just out of
campsite

Upon reaching El Rozario, you accept the fact that the giddy, two-beer buzz you cherished back in the States now takes five. Your flannel shirt and jeans have become your napkin, your washrag—they're smeared with car grease, speckled with salsa droppings, blackened from fire coals. You smell of sweat, diesel fuel, stale beer, and wood smoke.

Like all things superficial, your manners have fallen by the wayside. You feed yourself with dirty hands. You talk with your mouth full. No longer do you walk off yonder to relieve yourself. Instead, you stand up, take two steps away from the campfire and piss—a beer in hand, still talking. To blow your nose, you don't reach for a tissue. You simply place a finger on a nostril, lean your head to one side, and fire away. The sound rings crisp in the quiet desert air. Proud as a parent, you smile, wiping your nose on your sleeve.

> You travel farther south.
> You sleep better under the stars.
> Your thoughts become clear.
> The days move slowly, effortlessly.
> You don't know the date or the time.
> But you do know the tide.
> You have forgotten where you came from, and you're not too worried about where you're going.

◄ Crystal with all the necessities.

Separated at birth. ▶

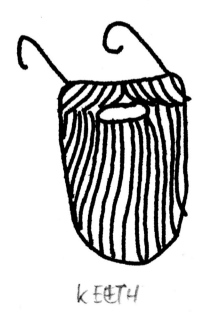

k EΘTH

▲ Elissa's art.

A Ride With Tim

Somewhere, about halfway down on a long desert drive, I hopped into Tim's truck. It's a '79 Toyota 4x4, rusted with chipped yellow paint and a funky camper shell. I had been in the Green Machine all day with the air conditioning on, so it felt good to have the windows down and the dry wind whipping across my face.

Casually, after a long period of silence, Tim said, "My steering wheel fell off."

"Yeah?" I said. "When was that?"

"Just back there at Escalera Nautica."

"What?"

"Yeah, I was pulling myself up into the cab, and it popped right off."

A nervous laugh leapt from my throat. Tim was sort of giggling to himself. The whole truck was vibrating as the worn cylinders maxed out in high gear.

"How is it now?"

Tim tugged on the wheel a few times. "It should be OK, just can't pull too hard. I could barely get my fingers in there to tighten it, but Keith said he has a wrench I can use at the next stop."

The sun was going down. Cactus shadows fell quietly across the desert floor, long and human-like. A full moon came into view—fake, as if held up by a string. Tim turned the stereo up. Willie Nelson's voice cracked lazily through the makeshift speakers. Surprised, as if they had suddenly appeared, I looked down at the cold Pacifico in my lap and the half a Vicodin in my right hand. I threw down the painkiller, chased it with a long swig of beer, and settled in for a long day on the road.

Reckless eighteen-wheelers with massive cattle grates, blind turns, steep shoulders, wandering burros, random obstructions beyond your wildest imagination. Add a bit of rain, some fog, and you have the most nerve-racking road conditions in the world.

Sitting on the plaster steps that lead to a shrine of Mother Mary in the back of Hotel La Pinta, Catavina, Baja. I'm writing letters. The best kind of letters are handwritten letters, not e-mails, that come from people in strange places who've strayed far from home. The age of computers has only made the written letter more precious.

Reaching what may have been the mid-point of the trip, after spending a few days camping in the desert, the five of us decided to treat ourselves to a hotel room and a hot shower. Last night we stood in the parking lot while Keith went in to get us a room. A few minutes later he walked out with his fists clinched and his face all twisted up.

"What happened?" I said.

"I was denied a room."

"What?"

"Yeah, as I walked into the lobby I saw the girl behind the desk reach up and turn the 'Vacancy' sign around to read 'No Vacancy.' I said, 'Can I get a room?' She said, 'Sorry, no rooms.' When I walked out, I saw her turn the sign around again."

I'd never seen Keith so pissed off. He was leaning against the truck shaking his head, hands stuffed deep into his pockets, clothes tattered and dirty, and that long beard of his. Somewhat of a vagrant.

"C'mon," I said, laughing. "Who ever gets denied a hotel room in Mexico?"

"I just did," said Keith, raising a hand.

We all burst out laughing.

I put on a hat and a sweater, clapped the dust off my jeans and went inside.

"Yes sir," she said. "How many beds would you like?"

MAIL

I'd been skunked on every previous surf trip to Baja—
always flat, windy, rainy, or all of the above. But this
trip was different. We just had a solid week of good
waves up north where a Mexican ranch owner told us
we were lucky. This time of year is usually, as he put
it, "No bueno."

Our minds were set on getting to the tip, but on a
hunch we decided to take a road out to the Pacific
side and have a look at the ocean. We'd stay the night
and move on. Again, our luck didn't fail. We ended up
posting up in a plywood shack for five days, riding fun,
head-high point surf.

Crystal finds a clean line ▶
protected by the after-
noon winds.

Dogs

CLOUD

Morning woke me. I was on the ground again, in my sleeping bag, my head under the truck. I kept my eyes shut, listening to the beginnings of day: the birds, a rooster, the waves. I could smell the coals from last night's fire still smoldering, with a haunting noise from a fresh crackling flame. It seemed odd to me that someone was up already, stoking the fire. Before I could process who it could be, I was overtaken by sleep.

I was soon awake again. That strange sound from the fire wouldn't leave me alone. I opened my eyes and saw the dirty underbelly of the gas tank, and the sky turning blue. A few stars still danced high above the horizon. That damn sound. I crawled farther beneath the truck, lowering my head to see who was tending the fire on the other side. I couldn't see any signs of fire, though, only smoke, and still that crackling sound. Then, in the half-dark next to the smoking coals, I saw something move. The figure was white and ghostlike. I rubbed my eyes and refocused. It was a dog. Oh yeah, I thought. Just Cloud, our neighbor's friendly pit bull.

The noise from the fire stopped. Cloud sat there smiling at me, wagging his stubby tail. After he realized I wasn't going to play with him, he dropped his head close to the coals and continued chewing on something. Then came that sound again. I scooted closer to see what was in his mouth. He looked up at me once more. Behind a twisting curtain of coal smoke I saw Cloud's head, large and distorted, grinning like an evil clown. Gradually, the smoke lifted, slowly unveiling an animal caught in the midst of brutal instinct. Hanging from Cloud's jaw, clinched between shark-like teeth, was a mass of raw meat. Luminescent viscera dangled in the dirt, blood dripping. Dilated dog eyes, black as death. Cloud was panting, drooling, and moaning. And beneath his chin, amongst splintered bones and shredded meat, stood a pile of curly white fur matted with blood. Flies circled the mess like tiny buzzards. Man, I recognized that fur.

A cute little poodle had arrived yesterday. She came rolling in on the dashboard of a brand new RV. Cloud was excited to have someone else to play with. He loves to play-fight with dogs from other camps. He lures them to a pile of palm fronds behind our shack

Cloud and Crystal.

where they engage in dog play: growling, biting necks, pawing heads, with occasional body slams against the plywood wall. But the poodle would have none of this. Instead, she preferred the front seat of the RV, where she sat all day shaking nervously in the heat of the windshield. Obviously an indoor dog, not fit for Baja—a snob perhaps. Cloud took great offense to this, and it was decided that she'd have hell to pay. Well, she paid all right.

I turned away from Cloud and looked out from under the truck, across the dirt to the ocean and the hills. The sun was rearing its massive head. I heard no waves. I lay down and dropped into deep sleep, welcoming dreams if they should come. That tragic crackling sound woke me again. I couldn't stand hearing Cloud ripping that poodle apart. So I rolled over in my bag and crawled under the truck to finally put a stop to it. It was fairly dark. The coals were still smoldering. I could see Cloud shrouded in a veil of white smoke. A light offshore breeze swept through. As the smoke cleared I saw that Cloud had a plastic potato chip bag in his mouth, his powerful jaw working it over like stale chewing gum. And beneath his chin was a pile of trash, pieces torn and strewn about, flies buzzing around. Cloud dropped the bag and stood there smiling at me, guiltily wagging his tail. I laughed and smiled back at him.

It's amazing how reality seeps into our dreams and vice versa. A potato chip bag turns into a dead poodle; waves turn into a train wreck; a sleeping bag becomes a cocoon. I turned toward the ocean, and Cloud went back to work. The sun was about to rise; a few stars were still out. I lay there with my eyes shut, listening again to the start of day: the birds, the waves…

▲ Keith.

Crystal. ▲

Crystal.

↑
leftover from ~~█~~ stamps.
Looks just like
where we are
now.

As Jeff says, Tim's truck
become a character on this
More like "cartoon" character.
It's cute, little. Rusted in all
the right places. And is the
perfect shade of 70's yellow
that you only get after years
being blasted by full-on sun
I think it's been here
in Baja before. I
wish it could talk.
... wish it could.
tell us where it's been.

← Talked to J. Nichols,
(marine biologist in Santa Cruz
before we left. He said to
keep an eye out for kids
wearing ocean revolution
bracelets. He and they? have
been handing them out when
they're down here doing sea
turtle conservation work.

tim's truck

'79 half ton
4 speed
4 wheel drive

ow.

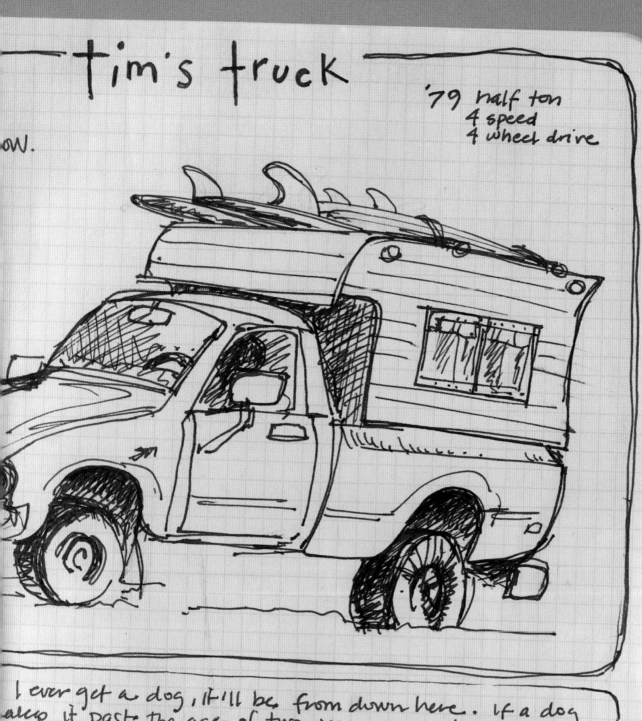

I ever get a dog, it'll be from down here. If a dog
also it past the age of two, you can pretty much
ssume it's both smart and lucky. And if it looks like
s not about to keel   over and die
mmorow, there's a good   chance it'll look
ce a show dog after a   few months of
eady love and good   food. Plus, the

-pat dogs I've met
ce they've had a   (baja dog) seem eternally grateful,
                                   taste of something else,
nd they're very happy to be with you.

grunion. these guys come completely out of the water
© to spawn on beaches. they're flipping around all over and
grabbable by hand. they spawn at night, after high tide for
3 or 4 nights following each new or full moon. The run lasts only a

topside is irredescent sapphire blue

body is translucent

tail is ultra delicate - like dragonfly wings.

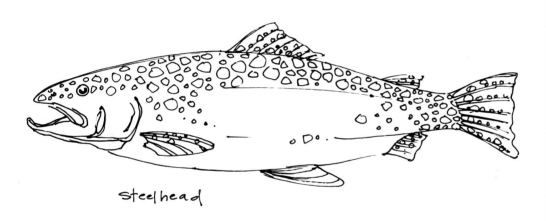

few hours, but thousands of fish may be on the beach at once.
The highest tides happen when the moon is full or new. Wave
action erodes sand from the beach, as the tide rises and
deposits sand as the tide falls — and grunions run at the falling
tide. The ♀ deposits eggs in the sand and they're buried by the
falling tide's sand deposits. The eggs stay buried for 10 days...
when the next high tides erodes the beach — and the baby grunions
hatch.

steelhead

rooster fish

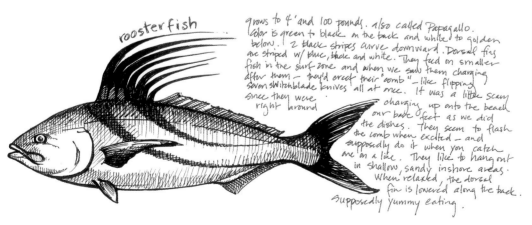

grows to 4' and 100 pounds. also called Papagallo.
Color is green to black on the back and white to golden
below. 2 black stripes curve downward. Dorsal fins
are striped w/ blue, black and white. They feed on smaller
fish in the surf zone and when we saw them charging
after them — they'd erect their "comb" — like flipping
seven switchblade knives all at once. It was a little scary
since they were charging up onto the beach
right around our bare feet as we did
the dishes. They seem to flash
the comb when excited — and
supposedly do it when you catch
one on a line. They like to hang out
in shallow, sandy inshore areas.
When relaxed, the dorsal
fin is lowered along the back.
Supposedly yummy eating.

MYSTERY SPOT
SANTA CRUZ, CALIF. · U.S.A.

CALIFORNIA
1V67667

Hmm...

Keith.

Once through the confusing checkpoint at Guerrero Negro, our two-truck caravan traversed to the gulf side of the peninsula. Winding down steep canyons, crossing sandy arroyos, getting sideswiped by eighteen-wheelers, we eventually saw the ocean again. Layers of greens and blues lapped up against the rust-colored mountains, a bit warmer, a bit dryer. The five of us stopped on a cobbled beach to stretch. All was quiet. We either stared out to sea or just sat, studying the ground. Occasionally one of us would point and mumble something, but only a few chose to look up. We began the trip with individual energies rising and falling independently. At this stage, it was as if we shared the same body: If tired, all were tired. If excited, all were excited.

▲ Tim and Crystal.

Keith having a rough morning. ▶

Somewhat lost.

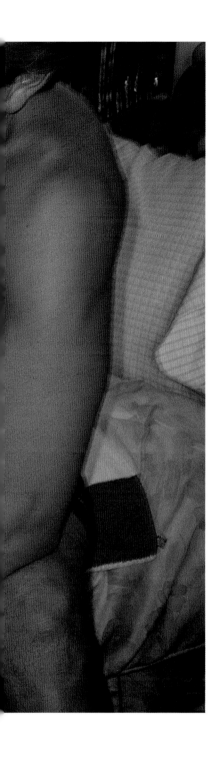

round stingray

I'd never seen anyone get worked by a stingray before. I'd heard horrible stories, but I still didn't think it could be that bad. In the first ten minutes following Crystal's stingray encounter, she complained of mild pain in her foot. After that period, it was a different story. Suddenly, it was as if one thousand volts of electricity surged through her leg. The next four hours were filled with muffled screams, violent shaking, and an endless flow of tears. I don't know how she endured that pain for so long. I would have passed out. Crystal is one of the toughest people I know.

Cabo!

Accidentally, we arrived on Easter weekend—the beginning of many spring breaks. The beach at Bahia Los Frailes was lined with local families from all over southern Baja: quad runners zipping up and down the beach, jet skis buzzing in and out of the surf, dirt bikes whining around. Tim and I explored the rocks around the tip of the point and decided to walk the beach on our way back.

The sun was setting; the inland ridgelines stood silhouetted in the deepening blood-red sky. There were a million tents lining the beach with families tucked inside, eating and playing games. Loud Mexican music poured from everywhere, fireworks blasted at random intervals. We walked past a large family sitting in chairs, not talking—facing the rear of the tent where a TV sat on a card table. Outside, next to their trucks, a generator pounded like a jackhammer through the smoke-filled air. Tim and I stood dumbfounded, in awe of what they were missing. Over their shoulders and beyond the tent was a stretch of soft white sand, little sparkling waves, and the brilliant yellow moon rising above the ocean like a prophetic apparition, a harbinger of times to come.

Tim downshifted to gain momentum on what looked like the onramp to the main thoroughfare connecting San Jose Del Cabo to Cabo San Lucas. Merging, shifting from second to third, we heard a car honk—apparently directed at us. It wouldn't let us merge. Instead, the bastard laid on his horn and stood his ground, forcing us to the shoulder. Then we heard sirens. From the opposite direction, an ambulance weaved its way through the stubborn traffic—not one car pulled over to let it pass.

I said to Tim, "They don't seem to have that sort of courtesy down here, do they?"

"Yeah," he said. "A little different attitude down here in Cabo. A much faster pace than up north where they have more dirt and more time on their hands."

We drove up a narrow side road and stood barefoot on an empty lot overlooking Old Man's and Zippers: totally flat but still a few guys in the water. Keith had his cell phone out and stared at it.

"What's up, Keith?" I asked.

"My cell phone works down here," he said, shaking his head. "Not a good sign."

▲ Crystal, fully recovered and in much warmer water.

▲ At one point, I saw Tim and the Chupacabra way outside the line-up. I looked through the lens and was appalled at what appeared to be happening. To my relief, I realized he was just giving it some air. Who would ever think of putting the air valve in such a place?

It was Keith's birthday the day after we arrived in Cabo San Lucas. To celebrate, I bought an inflatable Chupacabra. The poor little monster endured two days of humiliation and physical abuse, only to be abandoned one evening with very low self esteem.

In need of real greens, we were referred to an organic farm in San Jose Del Cabo. Owned and operated by American ex-pats Gloria and Patrick Greene, it is one of the largest suppliers of organic produce in the area. We were told that the southern peninsula of Baja produces 70 percent of the world's organic goods.

ORG. GARDENING

▲ Elissa.

▼ Patrick Greene.

The very tip of Cabo San Lucas. Back in the day, Yvon Chouinard did most of the first ascents down here. This was some of the dodgiest climbing I've ever done.

Arriving at the tip was a bit of a culture shock. High-rise hotels, tourist traps, traffic, shady characters offering us assistance with parking or, if interested, "Chicas baratas? Mota, si? Coca?" But we were only interested in seeing the tip.

A short boat ride through a flotilla of expensive yachts, drunkards on jet skis, and panga boats full of tourists, led us to a small, crowded cove. Our spirits were drained. This wasn't what we expected. But after walking to the other side, we were surprised to find no one around. And I was amazed that the entire peninsula of Baja California actually ends in a very defined tip. Pointing south, dividing the great Pacific Ocean and the Sea of Cortez, you have a finger made of sandy coves and bright white granite. It's Joshua Tree, California, meets Sandy Beach, Oahu—a climbing/bodysurfing Shangri-La. Keith enjoyed the splendors.

Keith forgot his harness on the tip. I forgot my swim fins. Keith slammed on the brakes and a huge bowl of salsa flew off the seat and landed in the gearshift boot—my fault, I forgot to secure it. Too lazy now to pull over, we dipped our chips in the boot for the rest of the drive. Signs began telling us the systems we had developed and trusted over the past six weeks were failing. The trip was ending. We had to get home.

▲ After waking up on a beach south of Todos Santos, Tim fills up the Green Machine with the last of our veggie oil supply.

Heading home.

▲ Stir crazy in Mulege.

Tim wishing his truck was vegetized. ▲

In the middle of the desert, somewhere near San Quintin, the truck suddenly died. Keith pulled to the shoulder and within five minutes we had all the gear out of the camper shell, and Keith was bathing in oil. Twice I saw a loose hose release a stream of hot veggie oil straight into his face. But Keith, with his newfound talent, prevailed and was able to jury-rig some tubes and get us a few more hours toward the border.

On this trip we ran the Green Machine on vegetable oil, biodiesel, and diesel, but eventually the truck would only cooperate while running on veggie oil. Before leaving Cabo we acquired bottles of store-bought Mexican cooking oil called "Cristal." In Ensenada, Keith poured in all we had left. Miraculously, it would be enough to get us home.

It was dark by the time we pulled into Ensenada. The truck was wheezing and gurgling as if fighting the effects of pulmonary edema. We had done the whole peninsula in two long days, and with the border less than two hours away we felt anxious, to say the least. All the stores were closed, so it looked like we would be sleeping in the Pemex parking lot. Then, five or six locals swarmed the truck, all offering a helping hand. One guy said his family owned a sewage-collection service. They had a yard full of car parts from old diesel pump vehicles. I jumped in his car and went across town with him. We spent about an hour in his yard under the hoods of ancient diesel rigs, ripping out old hoses and gaskets and rusty clamps. Back at the Pemex station, Keith and our new friends were able to jury-rig the thing once again. The wounded Green Machine limped across the border around 11 PM. We were home in Ventura by 3 AM.

The Crew

Keith Malloy is a former competitor on the World Championship Tour. He has since gone AWOL from the tour so he could grow a beard and drive his big green truck around. Highly energized at all times, Keith can be ready for a three-month surf trip in 7.3 minutes. However, if it has anything to do with work, he's guaranteed to be at least 12 minutes late. He was a finalist in the 2005 Pipeline Bodysurfing Classic, he placed second in the team division of the Molokai to Oahu paddleboard race, and in the fourth grade during a kickball game he booted the ball over the fence twice in one recess (the only other kid to do this was Roberto, who had been held back three times). Keith resides in Ventura, California, and is an ambassador for Patagonia.

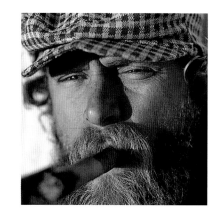

Dan Malloy grew up in Ojai, California, where he learned to surf on the beaches of Ventura County. After high school he spent most of his time in Hawaii, and he traveled and surfed in competitions around the world. After years of competitive surfing, "I couldn't quite cut the mustard," he says. "So I quit the contest circuit to help my brothers make films and to surf nice waves with no one around." Dan is the youngest of the three Malloy brothers and now lives in Ventura, California. He is an ambassador for Patagonia and can be found in their design studios when the waves are shitty.

Chris Malloy is the eldest of the three Malloy boys. At the age of 18, Chris left his hometown of Ojai, California and moved to the North Shore of Oahu, Hawaii. After a short stint living in the back of his car, he landed a pro gig chasing big waves and unridden breaks around the world. After fifteen years of non-stop travel (two months in one place being his record), Chris has re-claimed Ojai as his headquarters. Today, he splits his time between starting a family with his wife Carla, working with Patagonia as a surfing ambassador, and spending a ton of time in the water. When asked about his most prized possessions he's quick to answer, "A 10', 0" Tom Mobley, my spear gun, and an old grey ranch horse named Gilbert."

Gerry Lopez made his reputation at Pipeline, riding it like nobody else before him, or anyone since. He was among a crew of pioneers who first surfed Garajagan, or "G-Land," in Indonesia, which has long been considered one of the best lefts in the world. Gerry starred as himself in the surf-cult classic film Big Wednesday, and he was noted as 'shaper of the year' in Surfing Magazine's annual surfboard design issue for 2003. With his Zen-like approach to all things, regimen of two to four hours of yoga a day, and ability to surf and snowboard better than most teenagers, it is apparent that Gerry is just getting started. Not only is he an ambassador for Patagonia, he is an ambassador for inspired living. He lives with his family in Bend, Oregon.

Ivo Ninov was born and raised in Bulgaria and moved to America in 1999 without knowing a word of English. His dream was to climb big walls in Yosemite with the best climbers in the world. He has since done that and more. Teaming up with notorious members of the "Stone Monkeys," Ivo has made numerous record-speed ascents on El Capitan and has also established a few free routes around the States. Gradually, he has evolved into sort of a Yosemite Valley icon, carrying the torch for the dirt-bag climbing culture. He lives in Yosemite, Joshua Tree, Moab, Bend, Santa Cruz, Ventura, and so on. He's one of the toughest product testers for Patagonia.

Tim Nuanes is quiet and reserved and has the ability to appear and disappear without being noticed. He's a jack-of-all-trades and is incredibly resourceful, making him the ultimate travel companion. He is a cousin of the Malloy brothers, but doesn't like to admit it. Tim is reportedly still somewhere in Mexico.

Fletcher Chouinard is a true sportsman in the classic sense: He likes to fish, hunt, and exercise his athleticism through wave riding and running from the cops. He's a surfboard builder and an all-around craftsman—a bit of a renaissance man, but you won't find him discussing philosophy over a warm fire and a goblet of Port. For Fletcher, it's more likely death metal, Pabst Blue Ribbon, and not much talk. He lives in Ventura, California.

Scott Hulet writes, edits, surfs, and steers a family in San Clemente, California. Like Antonio de Fierro Blanco, he believes that since Alta California paved over its vaquero pastorale, Baja is the most dignified landscape a gentleman could hope to traverse.

Photo by Jeff Divine.

Crystal Thornburg was born and raised on Oahu, Hawaii. Her earliest memories are being pushed into waves at Waikiki. Just after the Bend to Baja trip, she graduated from Chaminade University with a bachelor's degree in environmental studies and a minor in art. An accomplished longboarder, Crystal is also an all-around ocean athlete. She is nationally ranked in Olympic flat water K-1 kayaking and is one of only two girls to compete in the annual bodysurfing contest at the Bonzai Pipeline. She is an ambassador for Patagonia and lives on Oahu's North Shore.

Brittany Griffith has been indulging in the life of a full-time climber for the past 12 years. She has climbed big walls in Yosemite, tackled 5.13 in both sport and trad routes on three continents, suffered in the cold in Patagonia, and covertly climbed in Cuba. If she's not out slaying men for sport she can be seen at the local bar drinking them under the table. Brittany's heroes include Julia Child, who attributed her longevity to red meat and gin. Last year, Brittany's accountant estimated that she spent 53 days at home in Bend, Oregon. She is an ambassador for Patagonia.

Elissa Pfost hails from the dynamic surf town of Santa Cruz, California, and she is the quintessential outdoor enthusiast. To earn money she works as a freelance artist and wordsmith. She's always on the move, constantly drifting in and out of contact. Rumor has it Elissa is still on the road.

Geoff McFetridge is an anomaly: a surfer, graphic designer, animator, filmmaker, textile designer, painter, silk screener, and furniture and product designer. Nothing is out of bounds as a means of expressing his creativity. Born in Calgary, Canada, Geoff now lives in Los Angeles.

Ben Lemke grew up in the hard-nosed coastal town of Oxnard, California. He comes from the school of hard knocks. At one time Ben was regarded as one of the local beach break enforcers—a punk-kid title he'll always deny. As a youngster he found a love for traditional longboarding and performed well in contests in both Hawaii and California. But don't pigeonhole him as only a longboarder, as the guy can ride anything well. Ben pursues his surfing passion by working for Patagonia and building surfboards with Fletcher Chouinard. He lives in Ventura, California.

Jason Frazier has nothing to do with this book, nor was he on the trip. We just think he's a legend right up there with Gandhi, Martin Luther King, Jr., and Uncle Dave. He has given us endless inspiration. Below is a copy of his business card (front and back).

• Photography • Used Cars • Land • Whiskey • Manure • Art •
• Surfboards • First Aid • Fly Swatters • Racing Forms • Rope •
• Literature • Bongos • Screen Plays • Harmonicas • Cigars •

Jason Frazier

• Wars Fought • CD's Burned • Happy Hours Made • Junk Restored •
• Revolutions Started • Golfers Ridiculed • Beers Quaffed •
• Assassinations Plotted • Bars Emptied • Trees Felled •
• Taxis Called • Governments Run • Orgies Organized •
• Uprisings Quelled • Women Wooed • Computers Verified •
• Jokes Told •

• Bargins Noticed • Tips • Flys Tied • Smoke Cleared •
• Spanish Butchered • Ideas • Mountains Scaled •
• Lies Told • Stories • Fish Cleaned • Fires Lit •
• Windows Rattled • Chains Pulled • Clocks Cleaned •
• Knives Sharpened • Heads Shaved • Crossbows •
• Maintenance • Gifts Accepted • Flaws Found •
• Supervision • Drinks Named • Tunnels Dug • BBQ •
• Dragons Slayed • Princesses Rescued • Steel Work •
• Sound Systems • Bullets Dodged • Directions Given •
• Honor Kept • Justice Served • Lost Dogs Returned •

ACKNOWLEDGEMENTS

I'd like to thank my parents for having me, dealing with me, not taking it personally when I ran away from home (I came back, didn't I?), and subsequently nurturing me into the person I am today. My Grandma for her humor, wisdom, the legendary rolls she makes on Thanksgiving Day and, of course, for having my mom, who had me, which was awesome, I'm sure. The Hopper family, because that's what my sister is now since she got married—a Hopper—and she and her husband, Mark, have the greatest kids in the world. You should meet them one day. Tammy Oliver for being one of my bestest friends in the world who has dealt with me through thick and thin and though she doesn't always listen to me she at least pretends to, and I appreciate that. Eddie Donnellan for reasons too inexplicable to put into words here on this small page in a language that is so ill advanced. Jesus Christ for having so much patience with all of us—don't worry JC, we'll get it right one day. Orlo Courtney Jones for being twice the man I'll ever be. Pollyanna Lind for her hard work and letting us crash on her couch. Lisa Polley, Adrienne Primosch, Jay Lamoureux, and Bill Boland for creating the Bend to Baja website. If you haven't seen it, check it out. Very cool. They worked their asses off to make it happen. Robert and Sharon at Casa Terra Cotta—if you're ever down in Cabo, look them up. They have a beautiful bed and breakfast and are always up for good conversation. Daniel Duane for popping in and out of our lives while on the road. Philip Drake and Mike Slone for without them this book wouldn't have been possible and the fact that Mike proudly drives a purple van gives all men who were on the fence at the local mini van dealer the confidence to go with the purple one. All my friends in Hawaii who I miss terribly and hardly see now that I have moved, and when I do see them they treat me like I never left and I like that. Ben Moon for helping us up the Monkey.

La Sportiva for making the best climbing shoes in the world. Coffee for all that taste and inspiration and giving us an excuse to sit around all morning sipping, thinking about all the cool things we could do but never really do. Tenacious D for coming out of the side hatch. Jane Sievert, Tim Davis, Sus Corez, Karen Bednorz, and Jeff Warner for helping me in the photo department—I'm an idiot, I know. The Star Lounge in Ventura for the cheap drinks, good company, and enlightened culture. Really, thank you. Helena Barbour for your support in all this craziness. Carla Malloy, Chris's wife, for keeping him in line. He needs that. Julie Ringler for dealing with the Malloys and me. Rob Bondurant for having faith. Rick Ridgeway for his guidance—I swear he's like Obi-Wan Kenobi educating us in the ways of the Force. Jim Davis (Brittany Griffith's housemate) for letting us party in his house and sleep in his yard. Buddha for his teachings and all the happy statues you see of him—big and small, made from wood or plastic or plaster of Paris or even rubber. Everybody should have one. I do. A few in fact. My favorite one is made of teak, and it sits next to my sink in the bathroom. On those rare mornings when I'm brushing my teeth after waking up on the wrong side of the bed, I look down at him and his huge belly and that giant smile, and it seems to help a bit. Erika Togashi for all the support she gave us while on the road. The Chouinard family for their commitment to alternatives and for always keeping an open mind. Charles Bukowski for never selling out, for his simple words, for lying, for telling the truth, for writing poetry I can actually read and understand. Hops and barley for all the good times... and the bad ones, too. Stuart Bjornlie for helping with the website video and for ripping, always ripping. And God for, well... everything.

- Jeff Johnson